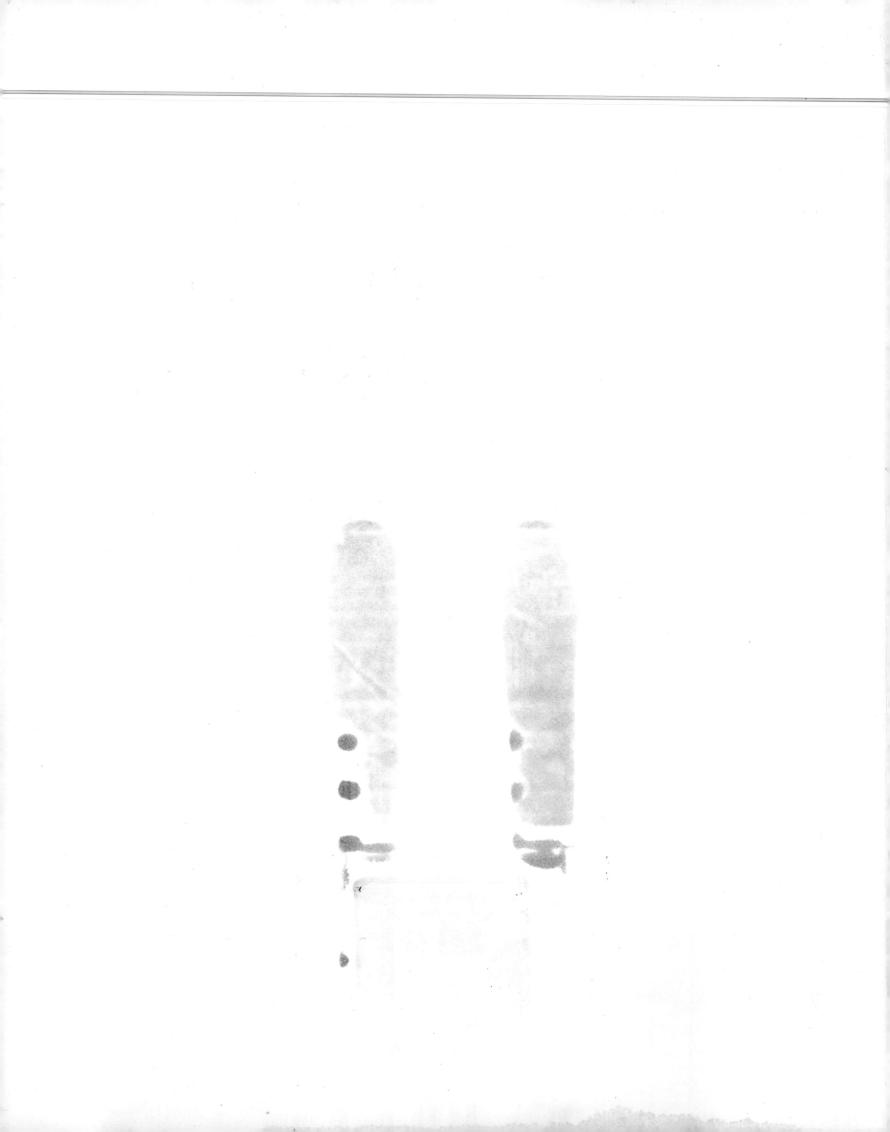

Great Buildings

The Nature Company Discoveries Library published by Time-Life Books

Conceived and produced by
Weldon Owen Pty Limited
43 Victoria Street, McMahons Point,
NSW, 2060, Australia
A member of the
Weldon Owen Group of Companies
Sydney • San Francisco • London
Copyright 1996 © US Weldon Owen Inc.
Copyright 1996 © Weldon Owen Pty Limited

THE NATURE COMPANY
Priscilla Wrubel, Ed Strobin, Steve Manning,
Georganne Papac, Tracy Fortini

TIME LIFE BOOKS
Time-Life Books is a division of Time Life Inc.
Time-Life is a trademark of Time Warner Inc.
U.S.A.

Vice President and Publisher: Terry Newell
Editorial Director: Donia A. Steele
Director of New Product Development:
Regina Hall
Director of Sales: Neil Levin
Director of Custom Publishing:
Frances C. Mangan
Director of Financial Operations: J. Brian Birky

WELDON OWEN Pty Limited
Chairman: Kevin Weldon
President: John Owen
Publisher: Sheena Coupe
Managing Editor: Rosemary McDonald
Project Editor: Ann B. Bingaman
Text Editors: Jane Bowring, Claire Craig

Art Director: Sue Burk
Designer: Lyndel Donaldson
Assistant Designer: Regina Safro
Visual Research Coordinator: Jenny Mills
Photo Research: Annette Crueger
Illustrations Research: Peter Barker
Production Consultant: Mick Bagnato
Production Manager: Simone Perryman
Vice President International Sales: Stuart Laurence
Coeditions Director: Derek Barton

Text: Anne Lynch

Illustrators: Kenn Backhaus; Chris Forsey;
Ray Grinaway; Iain McKellar; Peter Mennim;
Darren Pattenden/Garden Studio; Oliver Rennert;
Trevor Ruth; Michael Saunders;
Stephen Seymour/Bernard Thornton Artists, UK;
Roger Stewart/Brihton Illustration;
Rod Westblade; Ann Winterbotham

Library of Congress
Cataloging-in-Publication Data
Lynch, Anne, 1941–
Great buildings / Anne Lynch.

    p. cm. -- (Discoveries Library)

  Includes index.
  ISBN 0-8094-9371-3

    1. Historic buildings--Juvenile literature.
[1. Historic buildings. 2. Architecture--History.]
I. Title. II. Series.

  NA200.L96 1996

  720.9--dc20   95-32821

Manufactured by Mandarin Offset
Printed in China

A Weldon Owen Production

THE NATURE COMPANY
DISCOVERIES
L I B R A R Y

Great Buildings

CONSULTING EDITOR

Anne Lynch

Assistant Professor of History
University of Central Oklahoma, Edmond, Oklahoma

TIME
LIFE
BOOKS

Contents

• IN THE BEGINNING •

A Place to Live	6
Early American Empires	8
Early Civilizations	10

• THE CLASSICAL AGE •

Monuments to the Gods	12
Roman Recreation	14

• EMPIRES OF THE EAST •

Foundations of Religions	16
Spiritual Journeys	18
Center of the Universe	20
In Harmony with Nature	22

• EAST MEETS WEST •

Heaven Meets Earth	24
The Russian Heritage	26
Birth of Islam	28
Spread of Islam	30

• THE RISE OF EUROPE •

Starting Over	32
A Monastic Life	34
Royal Fortresses	36
Gothic Cathedrals	38
Monuments to Change	39
Grand Palaces	44
Age of Happiness	46

• THE INDUSTRIAL WORLD •

Reach for the Sky	48
Inspired by Nature	50
Adventurous Shapes	52
Games and Entertainment	54
A New Design	56
A Challenging Future	58
A Global View	60
Glossary	62
Index	64

A Place to Live

P eople must have shelter to survive. They will die without protection from the sun, rain, wind and cold. Today, people can live in almost every part of the world because they have learned to build walls and to put a roof over their heads. For centuries, people had no tools to cut or move trees and large stones, so the first houses were built from materials that were easy to handle, such as grasses, vines and small stones. They discovered that hard rocks with sharp edges could cut trees and other rocks, and these became the first building tools. Many centuries later, people melted metals from rocks to make stronger, sharper tools. In places with little stone or wood, people made sun-dried bricks out of mud to build their houses. Some of the earliest cultures in history were the first to discover and use many of the basic building materials still used today.

The roof
A waterproof roof is made from grass by thatching. Bundles of swamp grass are tied to a wooden frame so that each bundle overlaps the ones next to it and below it.

STONE HUT
Walls of stone shaped with tools surround clusters of houses in the village of Haaran on the Turkish–Syrian border. Each house has several rooms and each room has its own dome. Some even have a second story. Smoke from fires used for cooking escapes through holes in the roof.

MAKING BRICKS
Sun-dried mud bricks were perhaps the first synthetic building material ever made. A mixture of mud and straw is pressed into molds then laid out in the sun to dry, as seen here. The straw holds the bricks together so they do not crumble. As rain will dissolve sun-dried bricks, a coating of lime is added or a wide roof is built to protect the walls.

BEEHIVE HUT
This hut on Dingle Peninsula in Ireland looks like a beehive. It was built centuries ago by a monk who piled up small flat stones cleared from his fields. He stacked each circle of stones on top of the circle below and made each stone slope downwards slightly towards the outside, so rain could not get in.

The walls
Here a man is weaving mats from palm fronds or leaves, which will become the walls of his hut. Weaving stiffens the fronds.

SOUTH PACIFIC WOVEN HUTS
On the Trobriand Islands of Papua New Guinea, houses are still built from small trees cut with stone tools. The pieces of wood are tied together with vines to form the frame of each house. The island people use plant materials to complete the house. Grass and leaves bend easily and people thought they seemed too weak to use for building until they discovered how hard it was to pull them apart.

Discover more in Games and Entertainment

Early American Empires

The oldest architectural monuments in the Americas are found in present-day Mexico and along the west coast of South America. Early civilizations there had neither iron tools nor animals that could be trained to pull carts, yet the people constructed enormous stone buildings. The Olmecs and later civilizations in Mexico such as the Toltecs and Aztecs lived in scattered farm villages. These peoples had one religion and their religious centers were cities of stone such as Teotihuacán, where temples stood on top of tall pyramids. The peace-loving Mayan people lived in the rainforests of the Yucatan Peninsula in Mexico and they also built their religious centers of stone. In the fifteenth century, the Incas ruled an empire 2,480 miles (4,000 km) long in the Andes mountains of Peru. Their many towns were united by paved roads and a fast mail system. Incan stonemasons cut, polished and fitted stones together so tightly that a knife blade will not slide between them even today.

PALACE OF THE GOVERNORS
This palace in Uxmal, Mexico, is decorated with carved serpents and the Mayan rain god Chac. Religious leaders lived in its cool corbel-vaulted rooms.

Stairway of gods
Two sides of the pyramid have steep stairs. A row of carved masks of Chac, the god of rain, line both sides of the staircase.

PYRAMID OF THE SUN
This pyramid, built in the third century in Teotihuacán, Mexico, stands on a high platform and is surrounded by volcanoes. Stone covers a core of dirt and lava carried to the site by thousands of workers over a period of 30 years. Aztecs lived there centuries after its Teotihuacán builders had disappeared. They believed this pyramid had been built by the gods themselves.

PYRAMID OF THE MAGICIAN

The Mayans built this pyramid in Uxmal, Mexico, in the ninth century. It has an unusual oval shape and two temples at the top. The peoples of Mexico built high platforms, or pyramids, for their temples so they would be closer to the gods in the heavens.

At the top

The temples on the pyramid are stone replicas of Mayan thatched huts. Gifts were offered before statues of gods inside the corbel-vaulted rooms.

THE CITADEL

Offerings were placed on this Chac Mool, a god sculpted as a man lying on his back, which sits near an eleventh-century Toltec pyramid in Chichen Itza, Mexico. The pyramid has a steep staircase on each side and a temple at the top.

CORBELED ROOFS

A building constructed of stone posts and horizontal beams will collapse if the beams have to support heavy walls or if the posts are not set close enough together. Stone doorways and stone roofs or vaults, such as the one shown here, can be built with small stones called corbels. Each stone lies on top of the last stone and has one end sticking out over the opening. Once the stones or corbels from both sides of the opening meet at the top, stones placed on top of the roof will hold it in place.

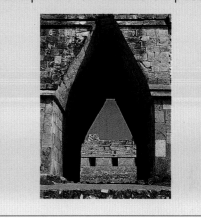

DID YOU KNOW?

The Pyramid of the Magician encloses three older temples. In Mexico, a new pyramid and temple often encased an earlier one. A completely furnished temple ready for use was discovered within the Pyramid of the Sun.

INCAN RUINS

Important religious ceremonies took place in Machu Picchu, an Incan town high in the Andes mountains of Peru. The plain stone walls of important Incan buildings were covered with plates of pure gold.

Early Civilizations

THE PYRAMIDS OF GIZA
These three pyramids were built more than 4,500 years ago as tombs for Egyptian pharaohs. The largest of the three, the Great Pyramid of Pharaoh Khufu, contains nearly two-and-a-half million stone blocks.

TEMPLE FOR A GOD
The huge columns of Egyptian temples still stand like stone forests in the desert above the banks of the Nile. This complex at Karnak was built over a period of 1,200 years. Here a statue of a pharaoh and his daughter stands outside the temple.

DID YOU KNOW?
Some Egyptian architects today are also building vaulted structures out of sun-dried bricks. The buildings stay cool and the materials do not damage the environment.

M ore than 5,000 years ago, a great civilization developed in Mesopotamia, the land between the Tigris and Euphrates rivers, then spread eastward along the north coast of the Indian Ocean. The Egyptian civilization developed beside the River Nile soon after. People traveled between the two areas and brought new ideas and inventions with them. Egypt had many workers and plenty of stone, and the Egyptians built huge pyramids and temples using simple tools and techniques. Because they did not have the wheel, 20 men pulled each stone to the pyramid on a wooden sled. Both stone and wood were scarce in Mesopotamia. The people there invented new materials such as bricks molded from clay and baked in an oven or dried by the sun. They then built wheeled carts to transport the bricks.

Steers and dragons
The symbols of the Babylonian weather god Adad and of the city's protector, the god Marduk, decorate the Ishtar Gate.

ISHTAR GATE

In the sixth century BC, King Nebuchadnezzar built a road called the Processional Way. This road led from his palace in the city of Babylon, the main city of Mesopotamia, to a ceremonial hall for New Year's celebrations. The Processional Way passed through the city's double walls at the Ishtar Gate.

PARADE OF LIONS

Every animal lining the walls of the Processional Way was brick, cast from special molds so that the bodies curved out from the wall. Each of the lions was made up of 46 specially molded and glazed bricks.

Arched vault

Buttress

Supports weight

INVENTING THE ARCH

A stone laid across an open space like a doorway is brittle and will break if a heavy weight is placed on it. To avoid this, the supports of ancient stone buildings were set close together. Mesopotamians invented the arch so they could build wide, open rooms. Bricks or small stones set in a curve form an arch. The weight of each stone pushes it against the next until one pushes against a thick wall, called a buttress. The buttress presses the stones together and holds the arch in place. A vault is a ceiling built with arches.

Glazed bricks
The bricks on the walls were painted with a glasslike mixture then baked to produce glowing colors.

An arched vault
The passage through the gate was 13 ft (4 m) wide, which was only possible because it was covered by an arch.

11

GREEK ORDERS

The Greeks built in three styles called orders. You can recognize the different orders by the style of the wide section at the top of each column, which is called a capital.

Doric order
This style has thick columns and plain capitals.

Ionic order
The thinner columns of this style are topped by a capital with two wide spirals called volutes.

Corinthian order
This order is more elaborate, and the capital is decorated with acanthus leaves.

Monuments to the Gods

In the fifth century BC, most Greeks lived in small city-states on islands in the Aegean Sea and in mountain valleys near its coast. The Greeks built temples as homes for their gods so the gods would live among them and defend their cities. The first temples were built of timber and sun-dried brick and looked like the Greeks own huts. Later temples were built on top of a three-stepped platform and surrounded by columns. When the wooden temples decayed they were replaced by stone temples, which looked exactly the same. The main goal of the Greeks was to make their temples look perfect. They built with the purest white marble and architects used geometry to design the temples so that all the proportions fit together in harmony.

TEMPLE OF ATHENA NIKE
The design of this small temple, dedicated to the goddess Athena, is based on a typical Greek hut. It was built in the Ionic style.

Under the roof
Walls and columns set close together hold up the timber frame for the tiled roof. There is little floor space in a Greek temple.

Frieze
A narrow band of carving encircles the top of the temple wall and shows the procession on Athena's festival day.

The goddess Athena
The tall wooden statue of Athena had an ivory face, arms and feet. She wore clothing made of gold plates that weighed 2,500 lb (1,134 kg).

12

CARVED IN STONE

The men and horses are part of a procession held every four years when Athens' leaders, warriors, athletes, musicians and poets climbed up to the Acropolis, on a bluff above the city, to present offerings before the Parthenon to Athena.

THE PARTHENON

After defeating invaders, the people of Athens built this temple between 447 and 432 BC to honor the city's patron goddess Athena, Goddess of Wisdom. The ruined remains of the Parthenon still stand within the Acropolis, Athens' original fortress.

ILLUSIONS IN STONE

The ancient Greeks knew that our eyes see temples differently from the way they really are. They used many tricks, called optical illusions, to create a perfect temple. If steps are built perfectly flat or horizontal, they will appear to sag in the middle. Every horizontal line in a temple, therefore, curves slightly upwards. If columns are built straight up and down, they will appear to lean outwards. The ancient Greeks built vertical lines to lean towards the middle.

DID YOU KNOW?

What has become of the plans drawn by the designers of ancient Greek buildings? A sharp observer recently found plans of one unfinished building carved on the inside of its foundation.

Stories in stone
This painted sculpture portrays dramatic events about the victories of Athena.

Colonnade
Athena's marble temple is surrounded by 46 Doric columns.

PONT DU GARD

The Pont du Gard is part of an aqueduct that carried water from mountain springs to baths and homes in Nimes, France, which was once a Roman city. The water channel stayed almost level as the aqueduct crossed mountains and valleys.

Take-out food shop and viewing gallery

COLOSSEUM

The 50,000 seats at the Colosseum in Rome stood on rings of concrete-vaulted passages, which were reached by stairs. Every spectator could leave the Colosseum in five minutes through exits called vomitoria. The Colosseum was used for many activities. It was flooded for mock sea battles, and gladiators tested their skills against lions that leapt into the arena when hidden doors snapped open.

Swimming pool
Every Roman boy was expected to be able to read and to swim. Baths in colder parts of the empire had indoor, heated swimming pools.

Frigidarium
The Frigidarium was at the center of the baths and was a popular place to meet friends. Four baths filled with cold water gave the room its name.

WORKING OUT

A mosaic on the floor of the baths in the Villa Casale, a private country house in Piazza Armerina, Sicily, shows women exercising. Many public baths had a separate bathing area for women.

• THE CLASSICAL AGE •

Roman Recreation

By the first century AD, Rome was a great empire. It reached from the Caspian Sea in the east and the British Isles in the north, to North Africa in the south. The Romans built roads with hard surfaces to connect their many cities. Aqueducts brought water to the cities from mountain springs. Luxury goods arrived in Rome's large harbors from every part of the known world. Romans in the cities bought food in take-out restaurants to eat in apartments with glass windows. They spent their free time watching plays or sporting events such as chariot races. They gathered at public baths to exercise and relax. Roman emperors ordered the construction of lavish buildings for public recreation to make themselves popular with the citizens. Roman engineers used synthetic materials such as concrete to construct these buildings, which were decorated with statues, mosaics and imported marble.

14

Tepidarium
Bathers took a dip in a basin filled with tepid (lukewarm) water to ease the shock of moving between hot and cold baths.

Caldarium
Bathers sat in hot tubs. Servants blended water from hot and warm cauldrons in the basement to keep the temperature at the ideal level. Cold water flowed from a fountain at the center.

BATHS OF CARACALLA
Emperor Caracalla built these baths in Rome, Italy, between 211 and 217. Gardens with sports fields, lecture halls and libraries surrounded the main building. As many as 1,600 people at one time could enjoy the swimming area, sauna, hot baths and the take-out shop.

Jogging track

Sauna
People sat on several tiers of seats in the dry heat of this sauna or in a nearby steam bath. The sauna was heated with air that was warmed over fires in the basement. The air passed under the floor then through tubes in the walls.

Gymnasium

Open exercise area

Changing rooms

MAKING CONCRETE

Romans made concrete from a mixture of lime, water and volcanic earth, which was poured over small rocks or broken bricks. The Romans built two walls of stone or brick then filled the space between them with the concrete. The walls and vaulted ceilings of the big recreational buildings were constructed from concrete.

Discover more in Games and Entertainment

15

SRI RANGANATHA
This tower in Mysore, India is one of 15 giant gateways through the five walls that enclose a Hindu shrine. The gateways were built between the eleventh and seventeenth centuries. The shrine itself is quite small and crowded by the priests' houses and the assembly rooms for pilgrims.

RANAKPUR TEMPLE
The Ranakpur temple honors Mahavira, the founder of Jainism. Jains believe that a person lives many lives, including those of animals. Jains try not to hurt any living creature. One of Ranakpur's large corbeled domes rises above the courtyard. The dome rests on two stories of columns and is surrounded by smaller domes.

• EMPIRES OF THE EAST •

Foundations of Religions

As early as 2500 BC, great civilizations flourished south of the Himalayan mountains, in what is now India. Three world religions began there—Hinduism, Buddhism and Jainism. All three teach that life, like a circle, has no end. It returns again and again as do the seasons. They believe that a person's soul comes back to live another life in a new body. This is called reincarnation. Hinduism began about 1500 BC. Hindus worship alone on most occasions, and many make pilgrimages to temples to pay homage to their gods. Hindu temples have richly decorated exteriors and pilgrims worship outside. The most important part of a temple is a small shrine with no windows, which is the home of the god. A tall, curved shikhara, or tower, rises above the shrine, and a series of open porches are used for assemblies and religious dancing.

BUILDING IN ROCK

In the second century BC, Buddhist monks built a monastery at Ajanta by cutting artificial caves into the cliffs above the river (left). Carvers chipped off unwanted rock and carried it away leaving a building behind. The columned entrance of the vihara (right), where the monks lived, led to a rectangular room surrounded by galleries. Each monk had a square cave that opened onto a gallery. Stone walls and ceilings were rubbed smooth then covered with paintings or carved with sculpture. The monastery also had a chaitya, or meeting hall, where people gathered to worship and study.

Shrine

Assembly hall

MYTHS IN STONE
The lively sculptures on the outside of Kandariya Mahadeo represent many of the figures in stories from Hindu mythology.

KANDARIYA MAHADEO TEMPLE
More than 1,000 carved figures cover this eleventh-century temple in Khajuraho. At first glance it looks like a mountain of rock covered with rows of sculpture. The temple stands on a high platform with the shrine under the tall shikhara at one end and a deep entrance at the other. Processions move through a passageway, which wraps around the halls and shrine.

TEMPLE FLOOR PLAN
Mathematical rules control the design of Hindu temples. Many small squares make up the floor plan of the temple. A square, which never changes, symbolizes the heavenly world.

Spiritual Journeys

Many different peoples live on the islands and peninsulas of Southeast Asia and they all have unique lifestyles. From early times, traders from all parts of Asia sailed along these coastlines and seaways. They traded goods and spread new ideas. Hinduism and Buddhism arrived from India, and Islam and Christianity came from further west to join the many local religions. Some of the greatest buildings in the area were built for Buddhist worship. Siddhartha Gautama, called the Buddha or the Enlightened One, founded Buddhism in India in the sixth century BC. He taught that every person could hope to achieve nirvana—a peaceful life beyond death where there is no suffering. Buddhists build stupas over relics of their spiritual leaders. A stupa is usually shaped like a dome and often stands on a square platform. Pilgrims walk along a path on the platform and meditate on the spiritual journey they will have to make to achieve nirvana.

BOROBUDUR
This Buddhist shrine has stood in a jungle on the island of Java in Indonesia since the beginning of the ninth century. It was built to look like a mountain. The stupa has eight stories or terraces. Pilgrims walk around each one on their way to the top.

ENTRY PAVILION
This magnificently carved gatehouse at Angkor in Cambodia leads to Angkor Wat, a twelfth-century Hindu temple. This temple may be the world's largest religious structure.

SMALL BUDDHAS
Statues of Buddha meditating under corbeled vaults line the corridors on the square terraces of Borobudur. The walls are carved with events from Buddha's life.

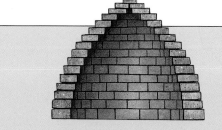

CORBELED DOMES

A simple corbeled dome is built by laying circles of stones flat on top of each other. One end of each stone juts out slightly over the room that is being domed. Pressure below and above one end of each stone holds it in place. A wide, heavy stone set on top locks all the layers below it in place.

At the top
A statue is hidden under the highest stupa.

ANANDA
This cluster of stupas in Pagan, Burma, partially hides Ananda, a white marble stupa rising in tiers above Pagan. This stupa shelters Buddhist relics.

WAT PRA KEO
The Royal Pantheon stands at the center of Wat Pra Keo in Bangkok, Thailand, the Buddhist area in the grounds of the royal palace. Ceremonies are held in the Royal Pantheon, which has eight gold statues of kings inside.

The goal
At each compass point, pilgrims can look up a long flight of steps and glimpse their goal at the top.

Discover more in Foundations of Religions

THE GREAT WALL OF CHINA

In the third century BC, the Chinese completed their first wall to keep out invaders from the north. This wall was rebuilt in the fourteenth century during the Ming dynasty. Five horses could walk side by side along the top. The wall still stretches for 1,500 miles (2,400 km) across northern China.

• EMPIRES OF THE EAST •

Center of the Universe

China is a unique country with a single civilization that has flourished for centuries in an area as large as Europe. The Chinese are known for their silk and porcelain and for their philosophies, Confucianism and Taoism. Philosophy and building have close ties in China. Both deal with how a person finds his or her place in the universe. Everyone is at the center of their own universe. A family's house marks the center of the family's universe. The palace of the Emperor stood at the center of China and of the universe as a whole. The Chinese were also influenced by other countries. Traders and travelers brought Buddhism from India along with Buddhist techniques for building with wood. Few ancient buildings survive today but we can still see what they looked like because important wooden buildings were later copied in stone. These buildings have elaborate wooden roofs covered with glazed tiles.

Bracket

Eave

BEAMS AND BRACKETS

The roofs of Chinese temples are supported by a number of crossbeams. They rest on short posts set on the beam below, so that fewer posts clutter up the floor. Each column has brackets on top. A bracket is like a pair of arms that reach out from the sides of a post. Each "hand" of the bracket supports a beam. Sometimes a bracket "hand" holds another bracket to reach even further out from the post.

TEMPLE OF HEAVEN
At the beginning of each spring, the Emperor prayed for an abundant harvest at this round hall with its three tiled roofs.

The Earth
The hall, like all important buildings, stands on a platform that represents the Earth.

20

HALL OF SUPREME HARMONY

The Emperor arrives at the Hall of Supreme Harmony in the Forbidden City. The hall was originally built in the fifteenth century during the Ming dynasty as part of the Imperial Palace. The building as it stands now was rebuilt in 1696 during the Qing dynasty. The hall and the Emperor's seat face south because the Chinese believe that a south-facing seat shows honor and respect.

THE FORBIDDEN CITY

The Imperial Palace was called the Forbidden City because few people were allowed inside its powerful fortifications. This 600-year-old painting shows government officials gathering outside the gates of the city.

The heavens
The wide eaves are turned up at the ends and seem to make the roof float above the hall. The elaborate roof of a Chinese building represents the heavens.

In Harmony with Nature

HIMEJI CASTLE
Castles were built for the nobility in the sixteenth century. Himeji, in Hyogo, has a tall central tower, or keep, surrounded by smaller towers linked by corridors. Soldiers, called samurai, defended the castle with guns and arrows.

DID YOU KNOW?

When early Japanese governments moved to a new capital, they ordered that the most sacred temples be taken apart, moved and reassembled at the new location.

The Japanese have learned to appreciate the beauty of natural things from a religion called Shinto—the way of the gods. Shinto teaches that simple things in nature, such as a tree or waterfall, may embody the forces of nature. The Japanese have also learned from the Chinese. In the sixth century, Buddhism reached Japan from China by way of Korea. Chinese and Korean carpenters brought woodworking skills with them, which the Japanese soon adapted to their own taste. The Japanese Buddhists also embraced the Shinto love of nature. Japanese wooden buildings are very delicate and have complicated details. Houses and temples are designed so they blend into nature, not stand apart from it. The people inside a building never feel cut off from the outdoors. A wall is often built so that it can be pushed to the side to open the room to a garden outside.

Brackets
These simple brackets make it possible to build this wall between the two roofs with just a few wooden posts set far apart.

Standing tall
A mast, which stands on a stone over the Buddhist relics, holds up this pagoda and its five wide roofs supported by brackets.

HORYUJI TEMPLE COMPLEX

These Buddhist temples in Nara were built in about the year 700 and are the oldest surviving wooden buildings in the world. This pagoda marks the place where symbolic Buddhist relics are buried and honored. The Golden Hall on the left shelters a statue of Buddha.

PHOENIX HALL

This villa in Uji opens onto surrounding gardens and pools. It became a temple of the Pure Land sect of Buddhists, who like to meditate in places that resemble the paradise their faith promises.

MADE TO MEASURE

For centuries, the Japanese have constructed buildings with standard parts made in just a few sizes. The distance between the pillars in a home or tea house fits the standard-size mats on the floor. The frame for each panel of the wall is the same size as a mat. Paper covers each frame to form a panel of the wall. These panels slide to the side to make two rooms into one or they open a wall to the outside.

Lever arm
A complicated yet beautiful system of interlocking brackets and levers makes it possible for posts inside the building to support the weight of the wide eaves.

Heaven Meets Earth

Christians believe in Jesus, the son of God, and their religion is based on his life and teachings. Christians were persecuted for many years during the Roman Empire, but in AD 313 Emperor Constantine made the religion legal. He then left the city of Rome and moved east to Byzantium and established a new Christian capital named Constantinople, which is now Istanbul in Turkey. The Roman Empire later split into east and west. The western empire collapsed after it was invaded many times by nomadic tribes from central Asia, but the eastern part survived to become the Byzantine Empire. Christianity as it developed there is called Orthodox Christianity. Hagia Sophia was the magnificent Orthodox church in Constantinople and it inspired builders of Orthodox churches for centuries. The great dome at the center of the church represented the heavens. The floor below represented life on Earth.

THE PANTHEON
For many years, the dome of the Pantheon, in Rome, Italy, baffled modern engineers. They did not know how the ancient Romans managed to build such a large dome. Then they discovered that the dome was made of concrete that becomes lighter as it gets higher because each level is mixed with lighter stones such as volcanic pumice.

DID YOU KNOW?
For many hundreds of years the dome of the Pantheon was the largest in the world. It measures 142 ft (43 m) across and is the same in height. Walls 16 ft (5 m) thick buttress the base of the dome.

A new technique
Byzantine architects learned to construct round domes over square rooms. They used four pendentives, triangles cut from a circle, to provide a round base on which the dome rests. The pendentives shift the weight of the dome to the four supports below.

THE CHURCH TODAY
Four towers called minarets surround Hagia Sophia. They were added when the Islamic Ottoman Turks, founders of modern Turkey, conquered the Byzantine Empire and converted the church into a mosque.

Central dome
The large, lightweight dome is built of a single layer of brick and is 107 ft (33 m) wide. It has a row of arched windows cut into its base.

THE CONGREGATION
There were no seats in Hagia Sophia. Worshippers stood in the space beyond the columns—the men in the aisle below and the women in the gallery above—to listen to the singing of the Orthodox church service.

Half domes
A half dome at each end lengthens the nave to 250 ft (76 m) and buttresses the main dome by pressing against its base.

DECORATING WITH MOSAICS

A mosaic is a design or picture made up of small pieces of colored glass or stone that are mounted on a wall or ceiling. Mosaics seem to glow in the dimmest light. At one time, many colorful mosaics covered the ceilings of Hagia Sophia. Jesus (right) and other great leaders and heroes of Christianity were portrayed in mosaics against a gold background, which symbolized Heaven.

HAGIA SOPHIA
Byzantine architects began this church in Constantinople in 532, during the reign of Emperor Justinian. They finished it six years later and it soon became the model for future Orthodox churches. The clergy, as God's representatives, met the emperor, the worldly ruler, under the great domes, where the teachings of Jesus were read.

Discover more in Monuments to Change

CHURCH OF THE NATIVITY

This church stands in an open-air museum of buildings near the city of Novgorod. Timber corbels support the gallery and demonstrate the remarkable skills of Russian carpenters. Although simpler in construction, it has much in common with St. Basil's.

Corbels

TRINITY ST. SERGIUS MONASTERY

Tsar Ivan the Terrible built the blue-domed cathedral for this monastery after the monks helped to fund his war against the Tartars. It was the most powerful of the Russian monasteries that were built inside fortifications, and it housed soldiers.

• EAST MEETS WEST •

The Russian Heritage

The first Russian people lived in the forests west of the Ural Mountains, where Europe meets Asia. Russian merchants traveled down the long rivers and across the Black Sea to trade furs with their powerful neighbor, the Byzantine Empire. They later adopted the religion of Byzantium and became Orthodox Christians. Mongol Tartars, nomads from Asia, conquered the area in the thirteenth century and ruled it for 200 years before the Russians succeeded in regaining their independence. In the sixteenth century, Tsar Ivan the Terrible attacked two Tartar states and took over their lands. He then set out to make Russia a great power. Russian carpenters were skilled builders of wooden houses and boats and learned from the Byzantines how to build with stone and brick. Both Russian and Byzantine churches have many domes, but Russian domes are mounted high above the roofs and shaped like onions to shed the heavy snow and rain that falls so far north.

THE KREMLIN

The city of Moscow grew out from this kremlin, or fortress. Palaces and cathedrals stand within its walls, as does a tall bell tower built by Tsar Ivan the Terrible.

DID YOU KNOW?

St. Basil's is named after Basil the Fool, a holy man who dared to criticize Tsar Ivan the Terrible. He was so popular that Ivan did not dare punish him.

A LOOK INSIDE

Frescoes of plants in colorful abstract patterns flow across the walls and ceiling of St. Basil's. These frescoes were rediscovered in 1954, hidden beneath layers of plaster.

Central tower
The tall towers in the center of early Russian churches were inspired by the high-roofed tents of the earliest Russians.

Onion domes
Eight colorful domes, each with a unique shape, surround the tower. Each dome crowns a small chapel.

ST. BASIL'S CATHEDRAL
When Tsar Ivan the Terrible conquered the Tartars he celebrated by ordering his architects to build a cathedral that would be a "hymn of joy." Construction on St. Basil's in Moscow began in 1554. This colorful building was originally painted white.

MAKING FRESCOES

A fresco painter spreads wet plaster on a wall or ceiling then paints it quickly so the paint sinks into the plaster before it dries. The only way to correct a mistake is to scrape off the layer of plaster and begin again. Sunlight slowly bleaches the color from frescoes, and moisture can cause the plaster to flake off. Shown here are frescoes painted on the outside of Voronet Monastery in Moldavia, Romania. They are unusual because they have survived the weather for more than three centuries.

Chapels
Access to the chapels is from a gallery around the cathedral, which is reached by two covered stairways.

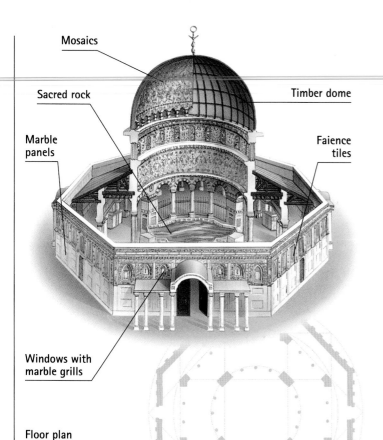

Mosaics

Sacred rock

Timber dome

Marble panels

Faience tiles

Windows with marble grills

Floor plan

DOME OF THE ROCK
This mosque in Jerusalem, Israel takes its name from the high dome built over a rock at a site that is sacred to Muslims. Pilgrims kneel to pray under the low roofs surrounding the rock. The mosque was completed in 691 and is the oldest surviving Islamic building. The decoration has been added in more recent centuries.

Birth of Islam

In the seventh century, Mohammed, an Arab trader, founded a new religion called Islam, which means "surrender to the one God." Mohammed urged his followers to care for the poor and weak. He spent his life teaching in the cities of Medina and Mecca and converted most Arabs to his beliefs by the time of his death. Those who believe in Islam are called Muslims, and they stop whatever they are doing five times each day to pray. A leader calls them to prayer from the minaret, or tall tower, of the nearest mosque, an Islamic place of worship. Mosques are decorated with flowing Arabic script and geometric patterns. Pictures of animals or people never appear on a mosque because Mohammed was determined to stop the worship of false gods. The tall, arched doorways of mosques and their high domes are often pointed or in the shape of a horseshoe.

Garden paradise
The tomb opens onto a garden because Mohammed, who lived in a desert land, pictured paradise as a beautiful garden cooled by fountains.

RESTING STOPS
Resting places for caravans were built along trade routes and in cities. Camels, donkeys and horses rested in the stables while merchants showed their goods.

PROTECTIVE TILES

Since ancient times, people in the Middle East have made tiles from baked clay. They glazed or covered the tiles with a mixture of liquid and glass and baked them again. These tiles were waterproof and were first used to protect sun-dried brick buildings from the rain. This picture is made up of faience tiles, which are tiles painted with pictures or other patterns before they are glazed.

THE MEMORIALS

A marble screen, carved to look like delicate lace, surrounds the memorials to Shah Jahan and his wife, who are buried below.

Call to prayer
Each minaret has a staircase that winds up to a balcony at the top of the tower. A crier calls Muslims to prayer from the balcony.

Double dome
An 80-ft (24-m) high dome sits inside the 200-ft (61-m) high pointed dome. The space between the two domes is empty.

TAJ MAHAL

Shah Jahan ruled an Islamic state in northern India. When his wife Mumtaz Mahal died in 1630, he built a magnificent tomb for her—the Taj Mahal in Agra.

Passing into the tomb
The tall doorway set deep in the wall is decorated with colored marble that is cut and placed together like pieces of a puzzle.

Tower of the Ladies

Hall of the Two Sisters

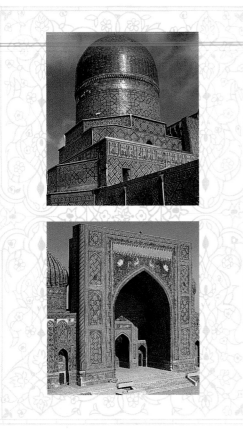

TALAKARI MADRASA

This high archway leads into an Islamic university, or madrasa, built in the seventeenth century in Samarkand, Uzbekistan. The dome rises over the mosque. Glazed tiles decorated and protected buildings, many of which were built of sun-dried brick.

• EAST MEETS WEST •

Spread of Islam

From the eighth century, the Islamic faith spread out along the trade routes. Islam reached China along with the camel caravans that brought Chinese jade and silk west along the Silk Road through Samarkand in the deserts of Central Asia. Islam spread along the north coast of the Mediterranean Sea where Arab traders exchanged Indian cotton and spices for glass and cloth to sell in India, where the new faith also took root. Strong Islamic states grew up along these trade routes. Rulers there built powerful fortresses on hills overlooking their cities. The luxurious palaces were designed to be cool during the heat of the long summers. They had large courtyards filled with colorful flowers, pools of water and fountains. The spray of the fountains kept the air fresh and cool. Shady rooms opened onto the courtyards and were separated from the outside by rows of columns.

COURT OF THE LIONS
Shaded walks surround this courtyard in the Alhambra. The fountain is surrounded by carved lions. The ruler held court in the Hall of Judgment at the end.

THE ALHAMBRA
The Alhambra, or red castle, was built in the fourteenth century on a high ridge above the city of Granada in Spain. Low buildings and garden courtyards form a palace at its center. Complicated geometrical patterns and religious sayings in graceful Arabic script are carved into the stucco on the walls.

CARVED DECORATION

Patterns carved into stucco decorated many surfaces. During this time, stucco was made from marble dust, wet lime and egg white. It was spread on a surface then allowed to dry before additional layers were added. The rows of small stalactites on the underside of the arch seen here were carved into seven layers of stucco.

Abencerrajes Gallery

Court of the Lions

COUNTRY ESTATE
The ruler of Granada also built a small country palace with large gardens. The royal apartments face the Canal Court shown here.

Court of the Myrtles

Starting Over

Life in the Roman Empire had become increasingly insecure, even frightening by AD 300, as entire nations of migrating nomads invaded the area. Christian worship, which had been illegal, was permitted in the hope that the Christians would convert the people of Rome and unite them to face the invaders. The first churches were rectangular buildings and could hold large crowds. The churches looked much like the Roman emperor's own imperial court, but the emperor's statue was noticeably absent. In its place was a mosaic of Jesus. These early churches were built with inexpensive trussed wooden roofs. Their stone columns often came from abandoned buildings and did not always match in height or style. The nomads gradually adopted Christianity and the religion spread out across Europe. People in the forest regions used wood to build their first churches, which resembled their pre-Christian temples.

Legendary beasts
Dragons, which the Vikings had always carved on their boats and houses, appear here on the gables of St. Andrew's Church. They are carved in wood and sit alongside the Christian symbol of the cross.

ST. ANDREW'S CHURCH
Built about 1150, this early Christian church in Borgund, Norway, is nearly 50 ft (15 m) high. Norwegians built churches the same way they built their boats. Flat boards, or staves, were attached to a wooden frame to form the walls. Here 12 tall masts support the highest of the three roofs. A second roof covers a low aisle and the lowest roof shelters the porch.

BENEATH THE ROOF
Triangles are used in several ways to strengthen the trussed roof of St. Andrew's against the wind and snow. Just under the peak of the roof, two timbers cross to form what is called a scissor brace.

TRUSSED ROOFS

A wooden roof built with trusses will span a wide room without posts in between. Trusses consist of triangles that are rigid because the angles of a triangle cannot change unless the length of its sides changes first. A trussed roof may form one large triangle or many small ones. The roof at St. Botolph's church in Norfolk, England, stands on two short beams called hammer beams, carved with angels. The wall holds one end of a hammer beam. A brace attached to the other end completes the triangle.

SANTA SABINA

This early church in Rome, Italy, was built shortly after the nomadic Visigoths captured the city in 410, destroying many buildings. This view across the church shows the Corinthian columns, which came from an abandoned building.

Jesus shown as a shepherd

Three kings bring gifts to the baby Jesus

COLORFUL MOSAICS

Early Christian churches were plain on the outside. But on the inside, the upper walls were decorated with mosaic portraits of great Christians and scenes from stories about Christianity. These mosaics are from early churches in Ravenna, Italy.

DID YOU KNOW?

Dragons are imaginary beasts that appear in the mythology of many different cultures and are found carved on buildings all over the world.

Discover more in Heaven Meets Earth

A Monastic Life

Religious communities lived in monasteries or abbeys and these were the chief centers of art and learning in Europe between the tenth and twelfth centuries. A single community often included several hundred men called monks, or women called nuns, who lived in a walled settlement. The monks and nuns divided each day between worship, study and work. Monasteries were often located in the frontier areas of Europe among various nomadic tribes. Monks built churches that looked like fortresses because they were seen as strongholds of God in an evil world. People came there seeking peace from the violence and wars around them. Living areas of a monastery opened off a cloister—a covered walkway built around a square garden. After the fall of the Roman Empire in the fifth century, many building techniques were forgotten. Stonemasons had to rediscover how to build arched stone vaults so the churches had fireproof roofs. These vaults were like those built by the Romans, so the style is called Romanesque.

SLEEPING QUARTERS
This dormitory in the abbey at the cathedral in Durham, England, has a trussed roof built from thick, roughly cut timbers. Light from large windows allowed the monks to read during their afternoon rest period.

Dormitory
In the winter, the monks sat by a fire in the warming room then went to bed in the unheated dormitory upstairs. A door in the dormitory led into the church because the monks worshipped in the middle of the night.

Refectory
Twice a day, monks sat down in the refectory to eat their simple meals.

Toilets

FEEDING THE COMMUNITY
On feast days, the monks roasted a wild boar over a fire in the center of the floor of this kitchen at Glastonbury Abbey in Somerset, England. They cooked other dishes for the large community over the four fireplaces in the corners of the room.

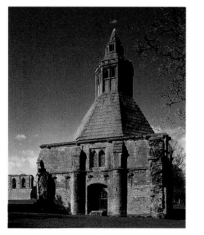

MAKING PILGRIMAGES

People rarely traveled in these times, but they did make a trip, or pilgrimage, to pray at the burial place of a Christian saint. Some pilgrims walked hundreds of miles to reach their goal, such as Santiago de Compostela in Spain shown here. They slept in monastic guest houses and prayed at churches along the way. Pilgrims brought home new ideas from their travels, including new ways to build churches.

Growing food
The monks worked in the fields of the farm outside the monastery walls. They also cultivated a small herb garden where they grew the plants used to make medicines.

34

Cellar
The monks made cheese and candles, cured hams and brewed ale to stock their cellar with all the things the community needed.

MARIA LAACH ABBEY
This twelfth-century Romanesque abbey west of Koblenz, Germany, has six towers decorated with dark stone. This scene reconstructs a typical monastery cloister next to the abbey church.

35

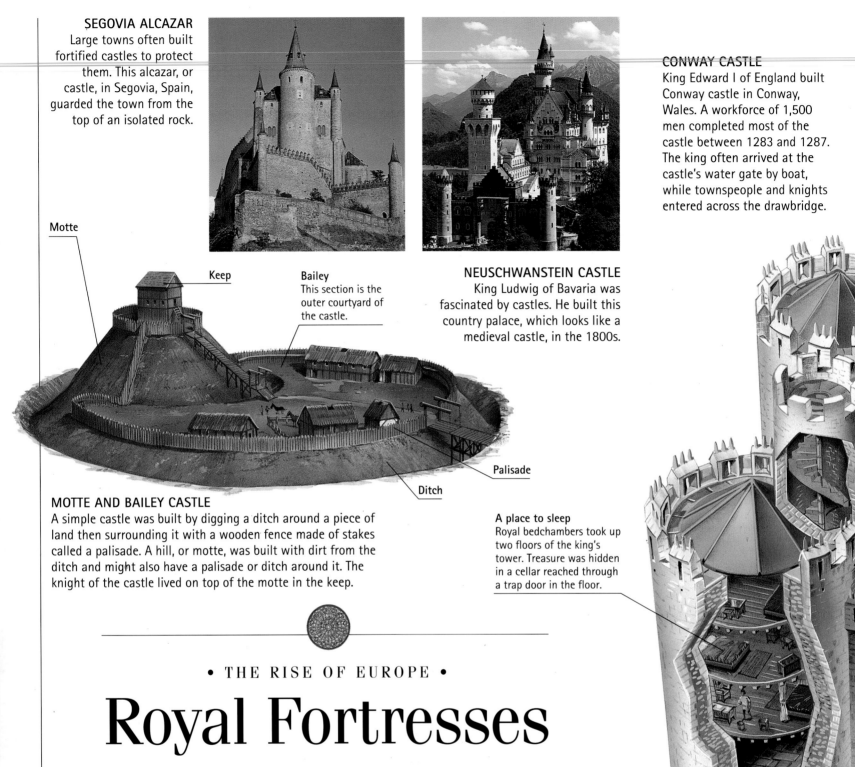

SEGOVIA ALCAZAR
Large towns often built fortified castles to protect them. This alcazar, or castle, in Segovia, Spain, guarded the town from the top of an isolated rock.

Motte

Keep

Bailey
This section is the outer courtyard of the castle.

Palisade

Ditch

NEUSCHWANSTEIN CASTLE
King Ludwig of Bavaria was fascinated by castles. He built this country palace, which looks like a medieval castle, in the 1800s.

CONWAY CASTLE
King Edward I of England built Conway castle in Conway, Wales. A workforce of 1,500 men completed most of the castle between 1283 and 1287. The king often arrived at the castle's water gate by boat, while townspeople and knights entered across the drawbridge.

MOTTE AND BAILEY CASTLE
A simple castle was built by digging a ditch around a piece of land then surrounding it with a wooden fence made of stakes called a palisade. A hill, or motte, was built with dirt from the ditch and might also have a palisade or ditch around it. The knight of the castle lived on top of the motte in the keep.

A place to sleep
Royal bedchambers took up two floors of the king's tower. Treasure was hidden in a cellar reached through a trap door in the floor.

• THE RISE OF EUROPE •

Royal Fortresses

For hundreds of years after the collapse of the Roman Empire in the fifth century, Europeans were often at war. Tribes fought tribes, and knights fought among themselves until strong kings conquered them. The first royal fortresses, or castles, were built of wood. The earliest stone castles were single square towers called keeps, built on high ground and surrounded by fences and ditches. As weapons changed, so did the design of castles. People built stone walls 16 ft (5 m) thick to shield them from battering rams, arrows, stones and a kind of burning tar. They filled their ditches with water, turning them into moats, so the enemy could not dig a tunnel under the wall and make it cave in. Archers positioned themselves in round towers that bulged out from the walls. This enabled them to fire their arrows on attackers from three sides.

A hasty exit
Prisoners were often taken to the dungeons of the prison tower through a hidden door in the Great Hall.

Great Hall
Banquets were held here and prisoners were brought before the king.

Arrow loops

Drawbridge

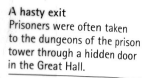

LIFTING THINGS

People and animals can lift very heavy weights without powered equipment by using levers. Here a page steps onto the long end of a board on a support called a fulcrum. His weight pushes his end of the lever to the ground and lifts the heavier knight a short distance into the air. The wheel that hoisted stone to the top of a castle tower also used the principle of the lever.

Repair work
A man climbed stairs mounted on the inside of a large wheel to wind a rope around a small wheel at its center and slowly lift stones tied to the end of the rope.

37

Cross
The top of the cross is 450 ft (137 m) above the pavement—higher than a modern 30-story building. It stands on a lantern, which was built to let light into the dome.

UNDER THE DOME
Worshippers gather around the altar, which is covered by a bronze canopy built in the Baroque style. St. Peter's tomb lies beneath the opening in the floor.

ON THE INSIDE
The interior of St. Peter's is decorated in the Baroque style. The nave is between the entrance and the altar. It is longer than the plan designed by Michelangelo.

Looking in
The dome seems to float above the interior. This effect is achieved because there are no supports directly below the dome.

Monuments to Change

ST. MARIA'S
This small church in Todi, Italy, built in the Renaissance style, was designed and decorated using only a few simple shapes. The architect Donato Bramante wanted St. Peter's Basilica in Rome to be a larger version of this church.

I n the 1400s, rich and ambitious citizens of Italy set out to create a whole new way of life. Their model was the civilizations of ancient Greece and Rome, which their scholars and artists carefully studied and copied. This period is called the Renaissance, and from Italy the movement spread to other parts of Europe. In the 1520s, Martin Luther called for the church to be reformed. He was joined later by other Cathol and Protestant thinkers such as John Calvin and Ignatius Loyola. Their religious activities produced the Reformation, which left European Christianity divided into many separate groups. The dramatic changes during these times inspired three new styles of architecture. While Renaissance architects built with simple shapes such as circles, squares and triangles, the new Mannerist style used complicated patterns to express the confusion of the times. The later Baroque style is recognized by its huge columns, bold curves, sharp contrasts and flamboyant and theatrical statues.

Bramante's plan

Michelangelo's plan

Dome
The dome is 140 ft (43 m) across and stands on legs 250 ft (76 m) tall. It is buttressed by chains wrapped around it. The dome is considered one of the greatest accomplishments of Renaissance engineering.

ORIGINAL DESIGN
The coin shows an image of St. Peter's based on the design of Bramante, the first architect for the church. Michelangelo later changed the original plan to include a wider and higher dome.

Gothic Cathedrals

GARGOYLES
The frog and mythical winged beast are called gargoyles. They are actually pipes that throw the rainwater away from the roof of the cathedral.

Wealthy European cities of the twelfth century built great cathedrals as residences for God and a place where citizens could gather in God's presence. High glass walls covered with stained-glass pictures surrounded worshippers in these buildings. Their builders thought of God as the light that showed them the way through life, just as the light of the sun revealed the holy teachings pictured in the colorful windows. Stonemasons built tall frames with thin stone supports to hold the glass walls. Stone ceilings of lightweight arched vaults often rose more than 120 ft (37 m) above the ground. Flying buttresses and other parts of a cathedral, which at first look like decoration, are actually part of the framework that supports it. Carved images of people, animals and plants decorate the frame. These new cathedrals pioneered a new architectural style called Gothic.

GOTHIC ENGINEERING
Gothic stone ceilings are made of arches and vaults that push, or thrust outwards. A buttress is necessary to keep the stones of the vault pressed together. These buttresses stand outside Gothic buildings and press against the vault inside by means of arches called flying buttresses.

DID YOU KNOW?
Everyone in a city helped to build the cathedral, which was large enough to hold all the citizens. On the way to the city, pilgrims also stopped at the quarry to help carry stone to the building site.

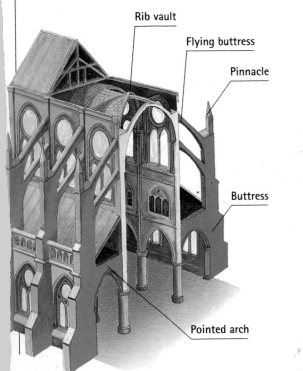

Rib vault

Flying buttress

Pinnacle

Buttress

Pointed arch

CATHEDRAL OF NOTRE DAME
Notre Dame's reflection can be seen in the Seine River in Paris, France where it was built on an island. Carvings of saints and angels surround the doors, which sit deep in the wall beneath tall towers. The cathedral was begun in 1163 and took about 150 years to build.

ST. PETER'S BASILICA

Eleven major architects directed the building of St. Peter's in Rome, Italy, which includes three different architectural styles—Renaissance, Mannerist and Baroque. Construction began in 1506 and took more than a century to complete.

Obelisk
Nine hundred workers and 240 horses moved this Egyptian obelisk across Rome, then stood it upright in the center of the piazza.

Congregation of saints
A row of 140 sculpted statues of saints and angels face the piazza from the roof of the colonnade—an evenly-spaced row of columns.

A COMPLICATED PATTERN
The front, or facade, of St. Peter's is designed in the Mannerist style. It has windows and doors in many different sizes and shapes. It is also wider than the church and high enough to partly hide the great dome.

DID YOU KNOW?

Vatican City is the world's smallest independent country. The Vatican mints its own money and also has an efficient postal system. Postage stamps often feature pictures of buildings, famous people and art treasures from the Vatican.

MICHELANGELO'S SISTINE CEILING

The Sistine Chapel, located in the Vatican complex, is the place where popes are elected. It is famous for the many frescoes on its walls and ceilings, which were painted by some of the most important artists of the period. Michelangelo always considered himself a sculptor, but he was also an architect, an engineer and a painter. He spent more than four years working on high scaffolding to paint the many scenes from Christian writings on the ceiling of the chapel. A figure from the fresco is shown here.

THE CHURCH OF ST. CHARLES

This church in Vienna, Austria has a wide facade, tall imposing columns and many flamboyant statues, typical of the Baroque style.

FAMOUS MASTERPIECES

This museum in the Vatican City was originally built to house Pope Julius II's collection of sculptures from classical antiquity. Many other popes added other ancient works of art. Works in many styles are now displayed.

Vatican Museum

Sistine Chapel

Piazza

Two arms made up of four rows of columns outline the piazza, the large open space in front of the church. The piazza is oval—the favourite shape of Baroque architects.

Vatican City wall

St. Peter's Basilica

St. Peter's Piazza

CITY WITHIN A CITY

Vatican City is surrounded by the city of Rome. The small walled town around St. Peter's is crowded with famous museums and palaces.

Discover more in Heaven Meets Eart'

42

THE SUN KING

Louis XIV, France's absolute monarch, chose the sun as his symbol. He believed his government was as valuable to France as the sun is to the Earth, where life is only possible because of the sun's light and heat. Scientists had only recently recognized that the sun and not the Earth was the center of the solar system. At Versailles, all roads and garden paths radiate from the palace, much like the rays of the sun.

HALL OF MIRRORS
The long, narrow stateroom in the Palace of Versailles has tall windows on one long wall matched by mirrors on the opposite wall. The bright sunlight and reflections moving across the mirrors dazzle the eyes so that it is hard to see what is at the opposite end of the room. This room inspired a hall of mirrors in every palace in Europe for more than a century.

A GRAND ENTRY
Rulers of small countries tried to look more powerful by building impressive palaces much like the Palace of Versailles. A coach pulled by four horses could drive right into this palace at Würzburg in Germany, where its occupants would descend and sweep up the stairs to the staterooms above.

Discover more in Age of Happiness

45

THE AMALIENBURG

In the 1730s, the ruler of Bavaria built this hunting lodge in the gardens of the Nymphenburg Palace in Munich, Germany for his wife Maria Amalia. A stairway led from her bedroom to her shooting terrace on the roof.

NYMPHENBURG PALACE

Three cube shapes linked by bridges make up this palace in Munich, Germany, which is built in the Baroque style. The Amalienburg is hidden among the trees to the right.

• THE RISE OF EUROPE •

Age of Happiness

The eighteenth century was an optimistic and light-hearted age. New ideas in science had convinced people that famine and disease could be conquered. Happiness was the highest goal in life. Statues of saints dancing or angels swinging from vines sometimes decorated churches. People no longer feared nature and they enjoyed the ever-changing plant and animal life around them. Some retreated from the busy city life to houses in the countryside. They invited friends there to enjoy the surroundings, listen to music, discuss science or play games. These country retreats were built in a delicate new architectural style called Rococo. Pink, yellow and other pastel colors made every room look cheerful. Rococo architects wanted buildings to look light and weightless. One way they achieved this was by covering walls and ceilings with delicate vines made of stucco—a type of plaster they could mold by hand into shapes. Stucco birds and butterflies flew across ceilings.

Hall of mirrors
Friends gathered for musical evenings in this round room at the center of the Amalienburg.

FOOD FOR THOUGHT
Maria Amalia and her friends could prepare their own meals in this blue and white kitchen. Each tile in the room has a different picture.

Kitchen

Resting room

Hunting room
Paintings of hunting scenes cover the walls of this picture gallery. Silver plant foliage made from stucco flows across the wall from one picture frame to the next.

DECORATING WITH MIRRORS

Glass was invented in Mesopotamia in ancient times. The Romans were the first to use glass for windows. In the seventeenth century, the French made plate glass by pouring liquid glass out onto a table and rolling it flat. Once the glass hardened, it was ground smooth and polished to make mirrors and large windowpanes. Mirrors often decorated the inside of Rococo buildings.

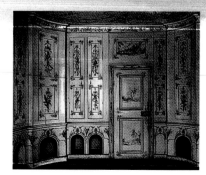

DE LUXE KENNELS
Hunting dogs slept in the kennels at the base of the walls in this room in the Amalienburg. Guns were stored in the cabinets above.

Discover more in Inspired by Nature

COALBROOKDALE BRIDGE
The world gained a new construction material when inexpensive iron was developed. In 1779, the English built Coalbrookdale bridge in Shropshire, which was the first iron bridge to be constructed.

DID YOU KNOW?
The first skyscraper was built in 1884 in the city of Chicago, Illinois. It was only ten-stories high.

EIFFEL TOWER
This iron and steel tower was built for the Paris Exposition of 1889. When radio was invented, the tower began its long career as an antenna. It carried the first transatlantic radio–telephone call.

Reach for the Sky

Skyscrapers are a product of the Industrial Revolution, which began in England in the eighteenth century. New inventions revolutionized the way people lived. Steam engines, and later electricity, made enough energy available to do many more times the work that people and animals had done before. A new method of smelting iron produced huge quantities at low prices. Other inventions gave builders steel, a material even stronger than iron. Cities grew and skyscrapers provided a solution to the problems of overcrowding because they take up little space on the ground. Skyscraper frames were first built with iron, then with steel. New engines powered elevators to hoist people to the top. The weight of a tall building can easily cause it to sink or lean, so the early skyscrapers were usually built on solid rock. This is why so many were built on Manhattan, a rocky island in New York City.

St. Peter's Basilica, Italy 1612	Great Pyramid of Khufu, Egypt 2700 BC	Eiffel Tower, France 1889	Empire State Building, USA 1931	Sears Tower, USA 1974	CN Tower, Canada 1976
453 ft (138 m)	479 ft (146 m)	984 ft (300 m)	1,250 ft (381 m)	1,453 ft (443 m)	1,804 ft (550 m)

THE TALLEST OF THEM ALL

For more than 4,500 years, the Great Pyramid of Khufu in Egypt was the tallest building in the world. Then the Eiffel Tower was built in France in 1889. In many parts of the world today, skyscrapers and towers continue to grow taller and taller.

Crown

The Art Deco style, a novelty of the 1930s, inspired the triangle-shaped windows. These are set within tiers of arches on the crown.

LIFE AT THE TOP

Native Americans were some of the earliest construction workers on skyscrapers. They worked at great heights while standing only on 8-in (20-cm) wide steel beams.

GOING UP?

Steam engines powered the first elevators, which were used only for freight. The first passenger elevators were installed in 1857 after a way was found to stop them from falling if a cable broke. By 1889, they were powered by electric motors. The elevator doors of the Chrysler Building (above) are decorated in the Art Deco style.

Core

A strong frame is built inside the building for the elevators. This frame also helps the building resist the pushing and twisting forces of the wind.

CHRYSLER BUILDING

Walter Chrysler built this 77-story skyscraper in New York City during the worldwide Depression of the 1930s. It provided much-needed employment for many construction workers. The building was the headquarters for his automobile empire and a monument to his success.

Inspired by Nature

THE PARIS METRO
The glass shell of the roof and the iron frame of this subway entrance are molded to look like the trunk and branches of a tree. This is just one of the many subway entrances in Paris, France, which were built in the Art Nouveau style.

New inventions had brought conveniences such as street lights and railways to many cities in Europe by the turn of the twentieth century. Railway stations, parks and houses were often built in an original new style the French called Art Nouveau or "New Art." Germans named it Jugendstil or "Style of Youth" and Spaniards simply said "Modernismo." Art Nouveau architects were inspired by nature. Stained-glass ceilings came alive with brightly colored birds and flowers, and the iron in balcony railings was twisted and tangled like vines. The Modernismo architect Antonio Gaudí copied nature by avoiding straight lines and right angles in his buildings, which seem to have been sculpted from lumps of clay. Such unique shapes were possible because the Industrial Revolution gave builders iron, steel and concrete to work with.

CASA MILÁ
In 1906, Gaudí began work on an apartment building, the Casa Milá in Barcelona, Spain. His friends said it looked like a wave that had turned to stone. Stables and parking for horse-drawn carriages were located in the basement.

BY THE SEA
Stairs curve up the lower wall of the two courtyards in Casa Milá. The apartment doors open onto the landings of the stairs. Gaudí designed the stairway to look as though it had been hollowed out by the pounding of waves from the sea.

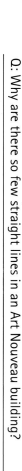

COME INSIDE
In this Casa Milá apartment, the walls of the parlor curve around corners and up into the ceiling. The ceiling was inspired by the ripples left by the tide in the sand.

Rooftop
Residents step out onto the roof terrace through stairwell exits twisted into crosses at the top. They can then wander through a rooftop landscape of fanciful chimneys.

SCULPTING A BUILDING

Art Nouveau architects rebelled against the practice of copying historic buildings such as the Parthenon in Greece. They studied nature and copied the shapes they saw there. The Belgian Victor Horta, a founder of Art Nouveau, imitated plant life in glass and metal. At Horta's Tassel House in Belgium, shown here, light from a colorful glass dome shines down on the twisted metal vines in the stairwell.

NOTRE DAME DU HAUT
The shape of the surrounding hills inspired the design of Notre Dame du Haut in Ronchamp, France. The Swiss architect Le Corbusier built this church in the 1950s.

Balconies
Casa Milá was inspired by the seashore. The iron guards on the balconies look like bundles of seaweed.

Discover more in Age of Happiness

FALLINGWATER

The architect of the Guggenheim, Frank Lloyd Wright, also designed houses that nestle into their natural surroundings. Fallingwater in Bear Run, Pennsylvania, copies the shelves of rock over which the waterfall beneath it flows.

GUGGENHEIM MUSEUM

The Solomon R. Guggenheim Foundation built its museum of modern art between 1956 and 1959 in New York City. The museum is constructed from a spiral of reinforced concrete in the shape of a hollow funnel. Its unusual shape contrasts sharply with the straight lines of the skyscrapers built around it.

New addition
A tower was added to the original museum in 1992. It provides additional office and exhibition space.

• THE INDUSTRIAL WORLD •

Adventurous Shapes

After the Second World War, many nations around the world made great economic recoveries. People felt confident and full of adventure. Architects of the 1950s and 1960s designed buildings with unusual shapes to reflect this new confidence. Some buildings have simple geometric shapes, while others look like huge abstract sculptures. Many of these structures could not have been built without the invention of a new material called reinforced concrete. A roof of reinforced concrete will bridge a wide room without any other supports in between. Steel and reinforced concrete are so flexible that walls and ceilings can be built into any shape. Sometimes the walls of a room or ceiling were built so they curved away from the people inside the building. This was done to give people a feeling of exhilaration—the spirit of the times in which these buildings were designed and constructed.

ROCK AND ROLL HALL OF FAME

This museum in Cleveland, Ohio, was designed by I. M. Pei and opened in 1995. It has rectangular bridges and circles and triangles of glass, granite and white-painted steel.

At the top
Museum visitors ride elevators to the top of the Guggenheim where they step out into the huge hollow shell of the museum. Sunlight from the glass dome floods down to every level of the museum.

ON EXHIBIT
Visitors to the museum wind their way down the long spiral ramp and stop to look at the modern paintings, hung on walls that lean outwards.

A BETTER BUILDING MATERIAL

Reinforced concrete is made by pouring concrete into molds around steel rods or wire mesh. This kind of concrete is no longer brittle, so roof supports can be set farther apart. Concrete reinforced with wire mesh is used to build thin, lightweight ceilings and walls and can be easily molded into any shape desired. The bowl shape of the assembly room in the Palace of the National Congress in Brasilia, Brazil (below), is possible because of reinforced concrete.

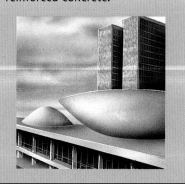

Walking on air
The reinforced concrete ramps have no supports below them at all. Only the walls hold them in place.

Discover more in A New Design

53

Keeping warm and dry
Spectators enjoy indoor comfort during Toronto's long, cold winters. The SkyDome's roof is in four sections and is made of a plastic fabric stretched on thin metal frames.

Tucked away
The half dome at the end swings on its rails around the side of the stadium and disappears under the other roof sections.

The best position
The two, arched, center sections of the SkyDome roof slide on rails to a new position at one end of the stadium.

• THE INDUSTRIAL WORLD •

Games and Entertainment

Since ancient times, people have gathered in large public stadiums or arenas for entertainment. Crowds still flock to these large buildings to watch sporting competitions, concerts and other special events. Many stadiums are open to the sky and spectators are at the mercy of the weather. They face the heat in summer and the freezing cold in winter. Events can be canceled if it rains or snows. But people in many countries no longer have to consult the weather report before an event, because some stadiums are now covered by roofs. The development of new synthetic materials, particularly plastics, has made these roofs possible. Tough, lightweight plastics are stretched tight on thin frames, much like umbrellas. These roofs, which come in many shapes and sizes, can cover even the largest stadiums. They shelter the crowds and the players or performers, and no-one's view is blocked by roof supports standing on the playing field.

SPORTS COMPLEX
Many large stadiums are built originally for special events. This stadium in Seoul, South Korea, was built for the 1988 Summer Olympic Games. It seats 100,000 spectators.

OLYMPIC STADIUM
Spectators in the Olympic Stadium in Munich, Germany, sit under a clear canopy of panels made from glass and plastic. The panels hang from a square mesh made of steel cable and are attached to cables that are stretched between 56 reinforced concrete poles and the ground.

54

THE SKYDOME

The SkyDome in Toronto, Canada, covers 8 acres (3 hectares) and includes a hotel. Several sections of seats move on rails to the best positions for watching each event. The grass for the playing field is artificial turf that is rolled out and zipped together with 8 miles (13 km) of zippers. This arena has a movable roof that can be opened and closed according to the weather.

Bird's-eye view
Twenty minutes later, the stadium is ready to welcome fans to the day's baseball game under summer skies.

Q: What makes the Toronto SkyDome different from other roofed stadiums?

ROOFING A STADIUM

Some of the largest stadium roofs hang from steel cables. As any tightrope walker knows, a cable that is stretched tight is as sturdy as a steel beam. A stretched cable is said to be under tension. Roofing made of glass and plastic can hang from steel cables stretched between poles and the ground to create a great tent such as the Olympic Stadium in Munich, Germany (above). Roof cables hold upright the frame of the J. S. Dorton Arena in Raleigh, North Carolina (below). The cables in the roof hold the arches of the frame up and the walls hang from the frame.

In 1957, a Danish architect Jørn Utzon won a contest to design the Opera House in Sydney, Australia. But it took him six years and the help of engineers and early computers to come up with a way to actually build it. Here the building is shown during different stages of construction.

Giant cranes
Three cranes arrived from France. Each required 30 trucks to transport it to the building site where they were assembled.

Roof ribs
Computers showed that the roof originally planned might have collapsed, so the design changed. The prestressed concrete roof was made by casting concrete pieces that were placed on the building before steel cables were threaded through them and pulled tight.

• THE INDUSTRIAL WORLD •

A New Design

The construction of an innovative building is difficult and often requires new techniques and special building materials. Many unexpected problems arise no matter how careful the advance planning may be. The architects and engineers building the Opera House in Sydney, Australia, faced major obstacles. The design was so innovative that it took several years for engineers to work out a way to actually build it. Specialists in sound, called acoustical engineers, advised on how the chosen building materials would affect the quality of sound. Metal, plastic and glass from around the world was used in the building. Manufacturers designed essential new equipment and construction workers learned new skills to build the Opera House. There were many unexpected costs and delays in construction. Sixteen years later, the architect's imaginative design became a unique masterpiece, which today is recognized throughout the world.

PRESTRESSED CONCRETE

The Opera House roofs were designed to be made of prestressed concrete much like the Trans World Airline building at Kennedy Airport in New York City, seen here. The steel in prestressed concrete is stretched tight so that it squeezes the concrete around it. The Trans World Airline building has a thin, lightweight roof, which was made by pouring concrete over a tightly stretched wire mesh.

Concrete sections
Each rib was assembled from concrete sections cast at the building site in reusable molds.

56

A GRAND PERFORMANCE

The audience sits on all sides of the orchestra in the Concert Hall of the Sydney Opera House. Acoustical engineers designed the rings that hang above the orchestra to reflect the music downwards so the musicians can hear how they sound together.

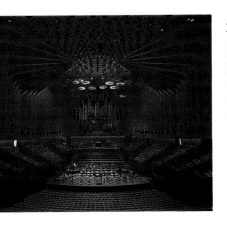

ON THE WATER

The Sydney Opera House stands on a small peninsula in Sydney Harbour. The roofs look like the sails of boats. The Concert Hall and the Opera Theatre are in the two large sections of the building. The small section is a restaurant.

Swedish tiles
Specially made tiles for the roofs came from Sweden. Workers attached panels of tiles to the roofs, which were assembled in advance on the ground.

Laminated glass
The walls and ceilings are made from curved pieces of laminated glass, specially made in France. A sheet of plastic was placed between two sheets of glass then heated until all three stuck together.

A night out
In 1973, the people of Sydney attended their first concert in the Opera House.

A Challenging Future

Large international corporations are building impressive and functional buildings. Many of these giant buildings are in California and Japan and other countries that border the Pacific Ocean. These areas are threatened by earthquakes that can shake buildings to pieces and destructive winds that can twist them apart. To protect the people inside, builders in these areas built low-rise buildings out of lightweight materials. As space became scarce, corporations needed high-rise buildings, so architects and engineers designed skyscrapers to withstand earthquakes. These now dot the skylines of many cities in the world. But buildings are not only threatened by natural disasters. Modern lifestyles also affect their future. Pollution from the fuel used to power cars and heat homes, for example, corrodes and weakens concrete. Each new generation of architects and engineers will face many new obstacles and technological opportunities. They will create different building materials, methods and architectural styles to meet these challenges.

HOW TO BEAT AN EARTHQUAKE

The TransAmerica Building in San Francisco is wide at the bottom and narrow at the top so that it will not topple over if the earth shakes. A high-rise building can also be built on top of a thick cushion made of rubber and steel, which absorbs earthquake shocks. Some buildings have steel tubes that push and pull the walls to keep them in their normal place even while the building shakes.

DID YOU KNOW?

Many perfectly sound buildings have been torn down because no-one could find a use for them. Today's buildings are more flexible. Even walls can be moved so a building can change as often as a business does.

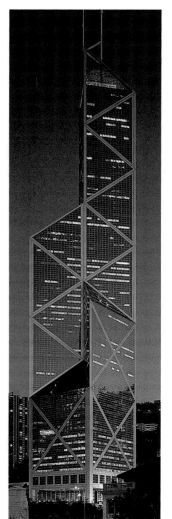

STACKING TRIANGLES

Destructive winds cannot twist Hong Kong's Bank of China out of shape because its frame is a series of rigid triangular braces. The bank blends into the sky, which is seen reflected in its mirror-covered walls.

CORPORATE MONUMENT

Lloyd's of London conducts its insurance business from this modern corporate building in London. Stairs, elevators and other services occupy the many towers, which surround a large atrium. People can escape by the stair towers on the outside if there is a fire in the building.

Executive lounge

Offices

Retractable glass ceiling

Wind avenue
Wind flowing down the building escapes through a wide vent so that people in the street below do not encounter the high winds created by most tall buildings.

Below the streets
The extra-wide parking basements of the NEC Supertower help the building to ride the waves of an earthquake, much like a ship rides waves at sea.

THE NEC SUPERTOWER

This corporate tower in Tokyo, Japan is narrower towards the top and looks like a space shuttle. The two narrow sections of the building contain 28 stories and stand on top of steel bridges, which cross an atrium at the center of the building. Blinds between the windowpanes lower automatically to protect against the heat of the sun. Hot air is sucked out of the building's exterior offices through the gap between the windowpanes and is recycled in other parts of the building.

A Global View

A great building can reflect many different ideas and styles and tells us about the beliefs and values of the people who designed and built it. You may not like the way a particular building looks or even understand why it is thought to be a great building. But once you learn about the lives and thoughts of the people who built it and about the time and place in which it was built, you may find something about the building that you do like. Throughout history, people have traveled from country to country, across waterways and mountains, carrying ideas about building with them. The pictures on this map show the locations of the major buildings that are featured in this book. But these are just some of the great buildings in the world. There are many others to discover.

St. Andrew's,
Borgund, Norway

St. Basil's,
Moscow, Russia

Notre Dame,
Paris, France

Palace of
Versailles,
Paris, France

Maria Laach Abbey,
Koblenz, Germany

Amalienburg,
Munich, Germany

Conway Castle,
Wales

E U R O P E

Toronto SkyDome,
Canada

Ishtar Gate,
Babylon, Iraq

Casa Milá,
Barcelona, Spain

Chrysler Building,
New York City, USA

Parthenon,
Athens, Greece

N O R T H
A M E R I C A

Guggenheim Museum,
New York City, USA

Baths of
Caracalla,
Rome, Italy

Hagia Sophia,
Istanbul, Turkey

Alhambra,
Granada, Spain

St. Peter's,
Rome, Italy

Pyramid of the
Magician,
Uxmal, Mexico

A T L A N T I C
O C E A N

A F R I C A

S O U T H
A M E R I C A

IN ANCIENT TIMES

Ancient buildings around the world looked different because they were shaped by the building materials available. Each material inspired a different construction method. People in the forest areas of Europe built in wood. Wood was scarce but stone was plentiful along the Mediterranean coast. The Egyptians there built great stone pyramids and temples, which still stand today. The ancient Greeks built their temples of white marble and the ancient Romans developed concrete to construct their huge buildings. The people who lived near the deserts between the Mediterranean Sea and the Indian Ocean learned to mold earth into bricks and melt sand to make glass. China and Japan built their early temples with timber. The brackets that supported their temple roofs were first used on ancient temples in India. Early people in parts of America used brick and stone as well as a type of concrete to construct their temples.

Hall of Supreme Harmony, Beijing, China

NEC Supertower, Tokyo, Japan

Horyuji Temple, Nara, Japan

ASIA

Taj Mahal, Agra, India

Kandariya Mahadeo, Khajuraho, India

PACIFIC OCEAN

Thatched hut, Trobriand Islands, Papua New Guinea

Borobudur, Java, Indonesia

INDIAN OCEAN

AUSTRALIA

Sydney Opera House, Australia

Glossary

Corinthian capital

Church of St. Charles, Vienna

SkyDome, Toronto

Vatican City stamp

Eiffel Tower,
Paris

altar A block with a flat top or table where offerings are made to a god.

aqueduct A channel built for moving water across long distances. It can also be a bridge that carries such a channel across a valley or river.

arch A curved structure built over a doorway or window.

architect A person trained to design and oversee the construction of buildings.

atrium A small courtyard completely surrounded by the rooms of a house, or a walled courtyard in front of a church.

bailey An open area inside the walls of a castle. A large castle may have more than one bailey.

beam A long, squared piece of wood, stone or metal that has a support under each end. The beams between two walls hold up the ceiling of a room or the floor of the room above.

bracket A piece of wood, stone or metal that sticks out from a wall or column to support a heavy object above it.

brick A molded block of clay baked in an oven so that it hardens and becomes waterproof.

buttress A structure that pushes some part of a building inwards to prevent it from moving outwards.

cable A strong, thick rope made from hemp or wire.

castle A fortified building designed to hold off enemy attacks.

chapel A room in a large building where religious services are held.

city-state A city, and the countryside around it, with its own independent government.

civilization A human society that has developed social customs, government, technology and culture.

column A tall, thin cylinder with a capital at the top and in some cases a wide, round base at the bottom. Columns are used to support a roof or the upper story of a building.

concrete A synthetic building material made from a mixture of cement, lime, sand, small stones and water.

corbel A piece of stone or wood that sticks out from a wall. A corbel is held in place at one end by pressure from above and below.

corbeled vault A stone ceiling made up of rows of corbels that rise from two walls and meet in the middle.

courtyard An area surrounded on several sides by walls or buildings and open to the sky.

dome A curved stone roof that covers an area the shape of a circle. Most domes are made from arches. Domes built with corbels are called corbeled domes.

faience A tile, brick or container made of earth that has been baked in an oven, painted with a design or pattern and then glazed.

flying buttress An arch in a Gothic building that connects a buttress outside the building to an arched vault inside.

fresco A picture painted on a wall or ceiling that is covered in plaster. The paint is applied while the plaster is wet.

frieze A decorative band around a wall. A frieze is most commonly used to refer to a band of carved decoration just below the roof or ceiling.

gallery A long, narrow room that is open on at least one side.

gargoyle A waterspout that is carved as a grotesque face or creature. It drains water from the gutters around the roof of a building.

glaze A liquid glass that is baked onto the surface of materials made from clay, such as pottery, bricks and tiles, to give them a hard, shiny and waterproof surface.

Industrial Revolution A change in the way people produced the goods they used. It began in England in the late eighteenth century. Engines powered by wood, coal, oil or water replaced much of the work once done by people and animals.

iron A strong metal used to make tools and parts of some buildings. It is found in certain types of rocks and is removed by very high temperatures.

keep A tall tower that is a castle, or the tall tower within a castle where the defenders retreat. The entry is usually high in a wall so it can only be reached by a ladder.

laminate To press or cement together several layers of materials, such as wood, glass or plastic, so that they become a single sheet.

lever A bar that rests at one point on a raised support or fulcrum. When the long end of the lever is pushed down, the short end of the lever on the opposite side will lift a heavy object a short distance.

marble A popular building stone found in many colors. It can be polished until it is as smooth and shiny as glass.

minaret A tall tower built outside a mosque that has a staircase inside and a platform at the top.

moat A ditch filled with water outside the walls of a castle. It is intended to keep attackers away from the walls.

mosaic A picture or design made by mounting small pieces of colored stone or glass on a wall, ceiling or floor.

nomads People who wander from place to place, usually in search of game to hunt or grazing land for their flocks.

obelisk A tall, thin monument that is pointed at the top and usually square at the bottom.

optical illusion When your eyes are tricked into seeing something that is not actually there. For example, you may be able to see a deep room in a flat painting.

pediment A wall shaped like a triangle that closes the end of a building between two sloping roofs. It is also the triangular decoration above a window or door.

pendentives Supports that make it possible to build a dome over a square room.

pilgrim A person who travels to a holy place. A pilgrim's trip is called a pilgrimage.

pinnacle A small peak that stands on top of a wall or a buttress.

plaster A mixture including lime, sand and water, which is spread on walls and ceilings and left to dry. It gives a smooth finish.

pumice A lightweight stone that comes from a volcano.

relic A possession of a person who was considered very holy, or a part of that person's body that is kept after death.

salon A French word for a room in a great house where guests are received and entertained.

scaffolding Metal or wooden platforms set up along walls or under roofs where workers and artists stand while constructing, decorating or repairing buildings.

shrine A structure people build over a place or object they consider sacred.

spire A tall, thin tower in the shape of a cone or a pyramid, which stands on top of a building.

steam engine A machine that changes steam into the energy used to power equipment and tools.

steel A strong metal made from iron and carbon melted together at a very high temperature.

stucco A smooth plaster applied to walls, which can be dyed, molded and polished until it shines.

synthetic Something that is made by humans and does not exist naturally.

tension The result of pulling or stretching an object. Building materials such as stone and concrete break easily under tension while wood, iron and steel remain strong.

terrace A level space that is raised above its surroundings. A building may stand on top of one or more terraces. The top of a building is said to be terraced if it looks like a series of steps.

thatch A covering for roofs made of bundles of straw, reeds or leaves.

tile A thin slab of baked clay. Tiles are used to cover roofs and floors and are often glazed. Glazed tiles were first used to cover buildings made of materials that water would damage.

tracery Frames of curved stone that hold the stained glass in the windows of Gothic buildings.

vault A curved roof or ceiling made of stone, which uses either arches or corbels.

Church of the Nativity, Novgorod

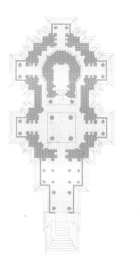

Kandariya Mahadeo floorplan

Colosseum, Rome

Lloyd's of London

Index

A

Alhambra, 30–1, 60
altars, 40, 62
Amalienburg, 46–7, 60
Ananda (stupa), 19
Angkor Wat, 18
aqueducts, 14, 62
arches, 11, 28, 30, 31, 34, 38, 43, 49, 62
Art Deco style, 49
Art Nouveau, 50–1
Australia, 56–7
Austria, 42
Aztecs, 8

B

Babylon, 10–11
Bank of China, 58
Baroque style, 39, 40, 41, 42, 46
Baths of Caracalla, 14–15, 60
Belgium, 51
Borobudur, 18–19, 61
brackets, 20, 22, 23, 61
Bramante, Donato, 39
Brazil, 53
bricks, 6, 7, 10, 11, 12, 30, 62
Buddhism, 16, 18, 19, 20, 22
Burma, 19
buttresses, 11, 38, 39, 43, 62
Byzantium, 24, 26

C

cables, 54, 55, 56, 62
Calvin, John, 39
Cambodia, 18
Canada, 48, 54–5
carvings, 12, 13, 16, 17, 19, 38
Casa Milá, 50–1, 60
castles, 22, 30–1, 36–7, 62
cathedrals, 26, 27, 34, 38, 43
chapels, 27, 42, 44, 62
China, 20–1, 61
Christianity, 18, 24, 26, 32, 39
Chrysler Building, 49, 60
churches, 24–5, 26, 27, 32–3, 35, 39, 42, 51 *see also* cathedrals
Church of St. Charles, 42
Church of the Nativity, 26
Citadel, 9
CN Tower, 48
Coalbrookdale Bridge, 48
Colosseum, 14
columns, 12–13, 30, 33, 39, 41, 62
concrete, 14, 15, 24, 52, 53, 54, 56, 62

Confucianism, 20
Constantinople, 24–5
Conway Castle, 36–7, 60
corbeled vaults, 8, 9, 19, 62
corbels, 9, 16, 19, 26, 62
Corinthian order, 12, 33

D–F

Dome of the Rock, 28
domes, 7, 16, 19, 24–5, 26, 28, 29, 39–40, 53, 62
Doric order, 12, 13
drawbridges, 36, 37
earthquakes, 58, 59
Egypt, 10, 48, 61
Eiffel Tower, 48
Empire State Building, 48
England, 33, 34, 43, 48, 58
faience, 28, 62
Falling Water, 52
flying buttresses, 38, 43, 62
Forbidden City, 21
France, 38, 43, 44–5, 48, 50, 51
frescoes, 26, 27, 42
friezes, 12, 62

G–H

gargoyles, 38, 62
Gaudí, Antonio, 50
Germany, 34–5, 36, 45, 46–7, 52, 54, 55
glass, 38, 43, 47, 50, 51, 53, 57
Glastonbury Abbey, 34
Gothic cathedrals, 38, 43
Great Pyramid of Khufu, 10, 48
Great Wall of China, 20
Greece, 12–13, 61
Guggenheim Museum, 52–3, 60
Hagia Sophia, 24–5, 60
Hall of Supreme Harmony, 20–1
Himeji Castle, 22
Hinduism, 16, 17, 18
Hong Kong, 58
Horta, Victor, 51
Horyuji Temple, 22–3, 61

I–K

Imperial Palace, 20–1
Incas, 8, 9
India, 16–17, 28–9, 30, 61
Indonesia, 18–19
Industrial Revolution, 48, 50, 62
Ionic order, 12
iron, 43, 48, 62
Ishtar Gate, 10–11, 60
Islam, 18, 28–31

Israel, 28
Italy, 14–15, 24, 32, 33, 39–42, 48
Ivan the Terrible, 26, 27
Jainism, 16
Japan, 22–3, 58, 59, 61
Kandariya Mahadeo, 17, 61
Karnak, 10
keeps, 22, 36, 63
Kremlin, 26

L–M

Le Corbusier, 51
levers, 23, 37, 63
Lloyd's of London, 58
Louis XIV, 44, 45
Loyola, Ignatius, 39
Luther, Martin, 39
Mannerist style, 39, 41
marble, 12, 14, 19, 28, 29, 61, 63
Maria Laach Abbey, 34–5, 60
Mayans, 8, 9
Mesopotamia, 10, 11, 47
Mexico, 8–9
Michelangelo, 39, 40, 42
minarets, 24, 28, 29, 63
mirrors, 44–5, 47, 58
Mohammed, 28
monasteries, 16, 26, 27, 34–5
mosaics, 14, 25, 28, 32, 33, 63
mosques, 24, 28, 30
museums, 52–3

N–O

Nebuchadnezzar, 11
NEC Supertower, 59, 61
Neuschwanstein Castle, 36–7
nomads, 32, 34, 54, 63
Norway, 32–3
Notre Dame, 38, 43, 60
Notre Dame du Haut, 51
Nymphenburg Palace, 46
Olmecs, 8

P

pagodas, 23
Palace of the Governors, 8
Palace of the National Congress, 53
Palace of Versailles, 44–5, 60
palaces, 30–1, 44–5, 46
Pantheon, 24
Papua New Guinea, 6–7
Paris Metro, 50
Parthenon, 12–13, 60
Pei, I. M., 52
pendentives, 24, 63

Phoenix Hall, 23
pilgrims, 16, 18, 19, 28, 34, 38, 63
pinnacles, 38, 43, 63
plaster, 46, 63
Pont du Gard, 14
prestressed concrete, 56
Processional Way, 11
Pyramid of Giza, 10
Pyramid of the Magician, 8–9, 60
Pyramid of the Sun, 8
pyramids, 8–9, 10, 48, 61

R

Ranakpur Temple, 16
Reformation, 39
reinforced concrete, 52, 53, 54
religion, 16, 18, 20, 22, 24, 26, 28, 30, 32, 34, 39
religious buildings/symbols, 8–9, 10, 12–13, 16–19, 24–5, 38–43, 51
Renaissance, 39, 41
roads, 8, 11, 14
Rock and Roll Hall of Fame and Museum, 52
Rococo style, 46, 47
Romanesque style, 34
Romania, 27
Rome, 14–15, 24, 32, 33, 39–42
roofs, 6, 9, 20, 21, 22, 32, 33, 50, 51, 52, 54, 55, 56–7
Russia, 26–7

S

St. Andrew's Church, 32, 60
St. Basil's Cathedral, 26, 27, 60
St. Botolph's Church, 33
St. Maria's, 39
St. Peter's Basilica, 39–41, 42, 48, 60
Salisbury Cathedral, 43
Santa Sabina, 33
Santiago de Compostela, 34
Sears Tower, 48
Segovia Alcazar, 36
shikhara, 16
Shinto, 22
shrines, 16, 17, 63
Siddhartha Gautama, 18
Sistine Chapel, 42
SkyDome, 54–5, 60
skyscrapers, 48–9, 58–9
South Korea, 59
Spain, 30–1, 34, 36, 50–1
sporting facilities, 14, 15, 54–5
Sri Ranganatha, 16

stained glass, 38, 43, 50
statues, 9, 10, 12, 13, 14, 16, 17, 19, 39, 41, 46
steam engines, 48, 49, 63
steel, 48, 52, 54, 55, 56, 59, 63
steps, 13
stone, 7, 8–9, 10, 11, 12–13, 16, 17, 19, 34–5, 36–43, 61
stucco, 31, 46, 47, 63
stupas, 18–19
Sydney Opera House, 56–7, 61

T–V

Taj Mahal, 28–9, 61
Talakari Madrasa, 30
tallest buildings, 48
Taoism, 20
Tassel House, 51
Temple of Athena Nike, 12
Temple of Heaven, 20
temples, 8–9, 10, 12–13, 16, 17, 18, 20, 22–3, 61
Teotihuacán, 8
terraces, 19, 51, 63
Thailand, 19
thatch, 6, 61, 63
tiles, 20, 28, 30, 47, 57, 63
Toltecs, 8
tombs, 28–9, 40
tools, 6, 10
tracery, 43, 63
TransAmerica Building, 58
Trans World Airline building, 56
Trinity St. Sergius Monastery, 26
trussed roofs, 32, 33, 34
Turkey, 24–5, 60
United States, 48, 49, 52–3, 55, 56, 58
Utzon, Jørn, 56
Uzbekistan, 30
Vatican City, 42
vaults, 9, 10, 11, 19, 34, 38, 43, 63
Voronet Monastery, 27

W–Z

Wales, 36–7
walls, 7, 20, 22, 23, 36, 42, 52, 58
Wat Pra Keo, 19
Wells Cathedral, 43
windows, 14, 38, 43, 45
wooden buildings, 10, 12, 20, 22–3, 26, 28, 32–3, 61
woven huts, 6–7
Wright, Frank Lloyd, 52

Picture Credits

(t=top, b=bottom, l=left, r=right, c=center, F=front, C=cover, B=back, Bg=background)
A.G.E. Fotostock, 50bl, 51tl. **AKG London**, 30tr, 40tr, 10tl (H. Bock), 24cl, 45br, 47bc, 50tr (E. Lessing). **Angelo Hornak Library**, 33tc, 43tc, 49c, 49tl, 56bl, 34tr (Courtesy of the Dean and Chapter of Wells Cathedral). **Arcaid**, 47tr (N. Barlow), 51tr, 54br (R. Bryant), 27cr, 27tr (M. Fiennes), 52tl (S. Francis), 58bl (I. Lambot). **Austral International**, 30tl (Camerapress/C. Osborne), 42tl, 62bcl (K.P. Head). **Australian Picture Library**, 54bl, 16cl, 36tl, 57tl (D. Ball), 49tcr, 49tr (Bettmann), 20bl (K. Haginoya), 10cl (D. & J. Heaton), 30tcl (B. Holden), 36tc (R. Price/West Light) 22tl (S. Vidler). **Bildarchiv Foto Marburg**, 47br. **Bilderberg**, 51tl (E. Grames), 50tl (M. Horacek). **The Bridgeman Art Library**, 34cl, 43tr (J. Bethell), 28bc (Courtesy of the Board of Trustees of the Victoria & Albert Museum), 45c (Johnny van Haeften Gallery, London), 44br (Lauros-Giraudon). **The British Museum**, 21tr. **Christine Osborne Pictures**, 7tr. **C.M. Dixon**, 31cr, 33cr, 38tr, 44cl,

44tl, 11tc (Berlin Museum). **Robert Estall**, 14t. **George Gerster**, 18/19c. **Timothy Hursley**, 52bl. **The Image Bank**, 58tr (A. Becker), 53tc (G. Colliva), 9br (G. Covian), 42c, 62tcl (G. Cralle), 41br (S. Dee) 45bl (G. Faint), 16tc (D. Heringa), 58br, 63br (R. Lockyer), 8cl (M. Martin), 26cl (H. Sund). **Magnum**, 19tl (M. Franck), 18bl (P.J. Griffiths), 40tc, 42cl (F. Mayer). **Jenny Mills**, 19br. **NEC Corporation, Tokyo**, 59c. **Nippon Television Network Corporation Tokyo 1991**, 42cr. **The Photo Library, Sydney**, 9tc (R. Frerck/TSW), 9cr (D.N. Green), 46tl (R. Smith), 20tl, 23cr, 34bl (TSW), 12tr (N. van der Waarden). **Robert Harding Picture Library**, 7cr, 19cr, 25tr, 48bl, 48tl, 57tr, 62bl, 26tr (G. Campbell), 8tr (R. Frerck), 17tr, 29tl (J.H.C Wilson), 7tl, 25br (A. Woolfitt). **Scala**, 16bl, 16br, 33c, 33tr, 39tl, 44/45t. **SCR Library**, 26br (D. Toase). **Sonia Halliday Photographs**, 24bc, 28bl, 43tl (L. Lushington), 17c (J. Taylor). **Werner Forman Archive**, 14bl, 31tl, 31tr, 13tl (The British Museum). **Michael S. Yamashita**, 23tr.

Illustration Credits

Kenn Backhaus, 60/61c. **Chris Forsey**, 12/13c, 12l, 13tr, 30/31c, 30tl, 36/37c, 36cl, 37cr, 62tl. **Ray Grinaway**, 2, 4/5b, 5tr, 17tl, 19tr, 20tr, 26tl, 27c, 39cl, 48cr, 63tcr, 63tr. **Iain McKellar**, 8/9c, 22/23c, 39–42c, 39bl, 42br. **Peter Mennim**, 3, 20/21c, 20tl, 32/33c, 32bl. **Darren Pattenden/Garden Studio**, 1, 24/25c, 24cl, 34/35c. **Trevor Ruth**, 54/55c, 54t, 55tr, 62cl. **Michael Saunders**, 50/51c, 52/53c, 53cr. **Stephen Seymour/Bernard Thornton Artists, UK**, 28/29c, 28tl. **Roger Stewart/Brihton Illustration**, 14/15c, 14cl, 15br, 63bcr. **Rod Westblade**, 4l, 10/11c, 11tr, 56/57c, 59tr, endpapers, icons. **Ann Winterbotham**, 5r, 38/43c, 38bl, 46/47c.

Cover Credits

Image Bank, FCtl, Bg. **Ray Grinaway**, BCbr. **Timothy Hursley**, FCc. **Sonia Halliday Photographs**, BCtl (L. Lushington). **Ann Winterbotham**, FCtr.